The ULTIMATE Book of Knit Afghans

Bobbie Matela, Managing Editor

Carol Wilson Mansfield, Art Director

Mary Ann Frits, Editorial Director

Kathy Wesley, Senior Editor

Sandy Scoville, Pattern Editor

Denise Black and Stephanie Hill, Editorial Staff

Graphic Solutions inc-chgo, Book Design

*For a full-color catalog including books
of crochet and knit designs, write to:*

**American School of Needlework®
Consumer Division**
1455 Linda Vista Drive
San Marcos, CA 92069

or visit us at:
http://www.asnpub.com

Thanks to the following:
   Solutia and The NeedleWorks for contributing afghans to this book

The NeedleWorks by Nancy J. Thomas is a newspaper column syndicated by
Universal Press appearing in newspapers throughout the United States.

Shown on front cover: Bobbles on Points

Patterns tested and models made by Angela Artale, Jane Bowen, Mary Ann Frits, Elaine Jordan, Sima Kashani, Eileen McNutt, Sandy Scoville, Susie
Adams Steele, and Kathy Wesley.

ISBN-10: 0-88195-936-7   ISBN-13: 978-0-88195-936-9   All rights reserved.   Printed in USA   16

Introduction

There's no better way to make a house feel like a home than by adding a decorator afghan made with love.

This book is your ultimate source for finding some of the best and most beautiful knit afghan designs of all time. You'll find many and varied designs—from classic to avant garde—all looking very in vogue in today's room settings. As you choose from our 19 afghans in this collection, keep in mind that you may change the yarn color to your own preference or to complement the room. The possibilities are endless!

Happy knitting!

beg .... begin(ning)
BC .... back cross
BL(s) .... back loop(s)
CB .... cable back
CF .... cable front
ch(s) .... chain(s)
CL .... cluster
dec .... decrease
FC .... front cross
FL(s) .... front loop(s)
gm(s) .... gram(s)
inc .... increase
K .... knit
K2 tog .... knit 2 together
lp(s) .... loop(s)
M1 .... make one
oz .... ounce(s)
P .... purl
PC .... popcorn
P2 tog .... purl 2 together
PSSO ... pass slipped stitch over
P2SSO .... pass 2 slipped
                stitches over

patt .... pattern
prev .... previous
rem .... remain(ing)
rep .... repeat(ing)
rnd(s) .... round(s)
sc .... single crochet(s)
SK2P ...... slip 1, K2 tog, PSSO
sl .... slip
sl st(s) .... slip stitch(es)
SSK .... slip, slip, knit
st(s) .... stitch(es)
tbl .... through back loop
TL .... twist left
tog .... together
TR .... twist right
T3B .... twist 3 back
T3F .... twist 3 front
T4B .... twist 4 back
T4F .... twist 4 front
T5B .... twist 5 back
T5F .... twist 5 front
yb .... yarn back
yd(s) .... yard(s)
yf .... yarn front
YO .... yarn over

* An asterisk is used to mark the beginning of a portion of instructions which will be worked more than once; thus, "rep from * twice more" means after working the instructions once, repeat the instructions following the asterisk twice more (3 times in all).

† The dagger identifies a portion of instructions that will be repeated again later in the same row.

: The number after a colon at the end of a row indicates the number of stitches you should have when the row has been completed.

( ) Parentheses are used to enclose instructions which should be worked the exact number of times specified immediately following the parentheses, such as "(K2, P2) twice."

[ ] Brackets and ( ) parentheses are also used to provide additional information to clarify instructions.

A Word about Gauge

A correct stitch gauge is very important. Please take the time to work a stitch gauge swatch about 4" x 4". Measure the swatch. If the number of stitches and rows are fewer than indicated under "Gauge" in the pattern, your needles are too large. Try another swatch with smaller size needles. If the number of stitches and rows are more than indicated under "Gauge" in the pattern, your needles are too small. Try another swatch with larger size needles.

Single Crochet Edging

Several of the afghans in this book have single crochet edgings.

A single crochet edging is worked as follows:

Step 1:

With specified yarn, make a loop on crochet hook with a slip knot. To do this, loop yarn as in **Fig 1**.

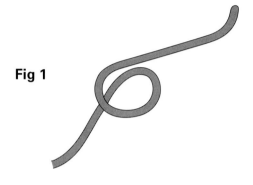

Fig 1

Insert hook through center of loop and hook the free end **(Fig 2)**.

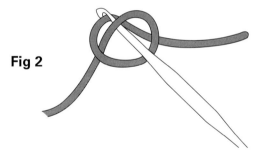

Fig 2

Pull this through and up onto the working area of the hook **(Fig 3)**.

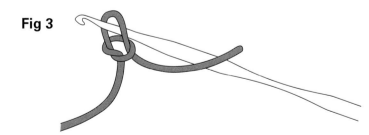

Fig 3

Pull yarn end to tighten the loop **(Fig 4)**.

Fig 4

Step 2:

To join with a single crochet stitch, with yarn at back of work, insert hook in stitch or space indicated from front to back **(Fig 5)**.

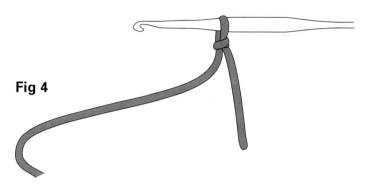

Fig 5

Bring yarn over the hook from back to front and hook yarn **(Fig 6)**.

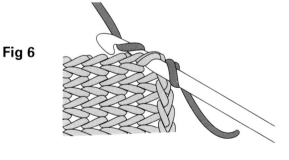

Fig 6

continued

Draw yarn through knit stitch or space and up onto the hook. You now have 2 loops on hook **(Fig 7)**.

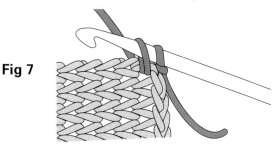

Fig 7

Again bring yarn over the hook from back to front, hook it and draw it through both loops on the hook **(Fig 8)**.

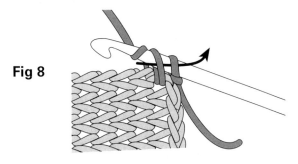

Fig 8

One loop will remain on the hook, and you have made one single crochet stitch **(Fig 9)**.

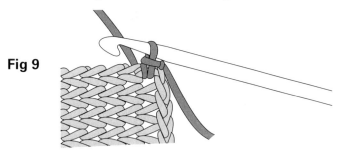

Fig 9

Step 3:
To work additonal single crochet stitches, work as follows:

Insert hook in next knit stitch or space as before, hook the yarn, and draw it through the stitch or space; hook yarn again and draw it through both loops on hook: you have made another single crochet stitch.

Continue working single crochet stitches as indicated in the specific pattern.

Step 4:
To work a second row of single crochet stitches, bring the yarn up to the correct height to work the first stitch, and then turn the work so you can work back across the first row. So to raise the yarn, it is necessary to chain 1. After completing the last single crochet stitch, bring yarn over the hook from back to front and hook it; draw hooked yarn through the loop on the hook and up onto the hook. You have now made one chain stitch **(Fig 10)**.

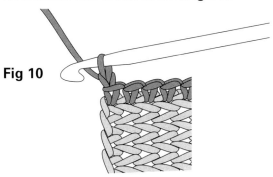

Fig 10

Now turn the work in the direction of the arrow (counter-clockwise) as shown in **Fig 11**.

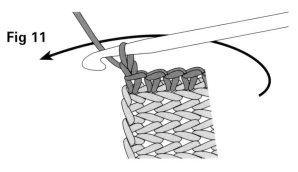

Fig 11

Do not remove the hook from the loop as you do this **(Fig 12)**.

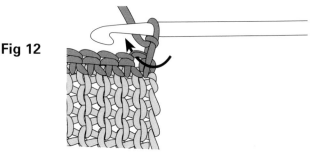

Fig 12

Insert hook under both loops of the previous single crochet stitch as shown in **Fig 13**.

Fig 13

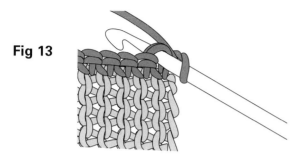

Work a single crochet stitch as before in each single crochet stitch to the end.

Step 5:

When working an edging around an afghan, it is necessary to join the last single crochet stitch made to the first one. To do this, insert hook under both loops of the first single crochet, hook yarn and draw it through stitch and through loop on hook. Now first and last single crochet stitches are joined.

Working With Pattern Charts

When working in rows, read odd numbered rows from right to left, and even numbered rows from left to right.

Odd numbered rows represent the right side of your work, and are usually knit. Even numbered rows represent the wrong side of your work, and are usually purled.

Duplicate Stitch

Duplicate stitch is an embroidery stitch that duplicates the "V" of the knit stitch it will cover. Duplicate stitch is often used when carrying yarns is not practical.

To work duplicate stitch, thread a 24" length of yarn in color stated through a tapestry needle. On wrong side of afghan, anchor thread by weaving the yarn away from and back toward location of the first stitch.

Bring needle up at base of first stitch and slide needle under both loops of stitch above **(Fig 14)**; insert needle down in same space at base of stitch **(Fig 15)**.

Following chart, repeat for remaining stitches. When last duplicate stitch is completed, weave through several stitches in both directions on wrong side to anchor yarn.

Fig 14

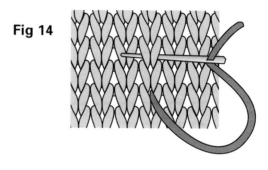

Fig 15

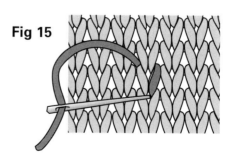

Fringe

Basic Instructions

Cut a piece of cardboard half as long as specified in instructions for strands plus 1/2" for trimming allowance. Wind yarn loosely and evenly lengthwise around cardboard. When card is filled, cut yarn across one end. Do this several times, then begin fringing; you can wind additional strands as you need them.

Single Knot Fringe

Hold specified number of strands for one knot of fringe together, then fold in half. Hold afghan with right side facing you. Use crochet hook to draw folded end through space or stitch from right to wrong side (**Figs 1 and 2**), pull loose ends through folded section (**Fig 3**) and draw knot up firmly (**Fig 4**). Space knots as indicated in pattern instructions.

Double Knot Fringe

Begin by working Single Knot Fringe completely across one end of afghan. With right side facing you and working from left to right, take half the strands of one knot and half the strands of the knot next to it, and knot them together (**Fig 5**).

Triple Knot Fringe

First work Double Knot Fringe. Then working again on the right side from left to right, tie third row of knots (**Fig 6**).

Spaghetti Fringe

Each knot is tied with just one strand of yarn. Use same knotting method as Single Knot Fringe.

Fig 1
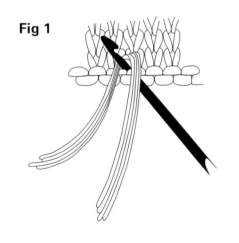

Fig 2
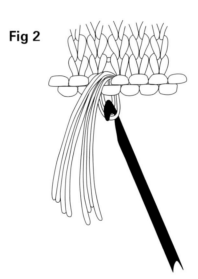

Fig 3
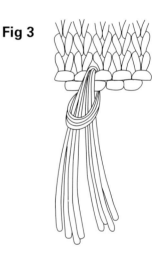

Fig 4
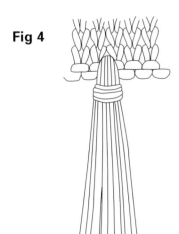

Fig 5
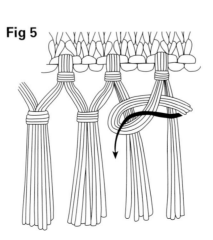

Fig 6
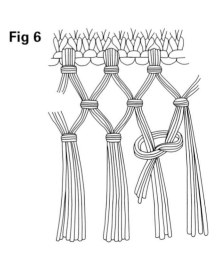

Metric Charts

INCHES INTO MILLIMETERS & CENTIMETERS (Rounded off slightly)

inches	mm	cm	inches	cm	inches	cm	inches	cm
1/8	3		5	12.5	21	53.5	38	96.5
1/4	6		5 1/2	14	22	56	39	99
3/8	10	1	6	15	23	58.5	40	101.5
1/2	13	1.3	7	18	24	61	41	104
5/8	15	1.5	8	20.5	25	63.5	42	106.5
3/4	20	2	9	23	26	66	43	109
7/8	22	2.2	10	25.5	27	68.5	44	112
1	25	2.5	11	28	28	71	45	114.5
1 1/4	32	3.2	12	30.5	29	73.5	46	117
1 1/2	38	3.8	13	33	30	76	47	119.5
1 3/4	45	4.5	14	35.5	31	79	48	122
2	50	5	15	38	32	81.5	49	124.5
2 1/2	65	6.5	16	40.5	33	84	50	127
3	75	7.5	17	43	34	86.5		
3 1/2	90	9	18	46	35	89		
4	100	10	19	48.5	36	91.5		
4 1/2	115	11.5	20	51	37	94		

mm - millimeter   cm - centimeter

KNITTING NEEDLES CONVERSION CHART

U.S.	0	1	2	3	4	5	6	7	8	9	10	10 1/2	11	13	15
Metric(mm)	2	2 1/4	2 3/4	3 1/8	3 1/2	3 3/4	4 1/4	4 1/2	5	5 1/4	5 3/4	6 1/2	8	9	10

CROCHET HOOKS CONVERSION CHART

U.S.	1/B	2/C	3/D	4/E	5/F	6/G	8/H	9/I	10/J	10 1/2/K	N
Continental-mm	2.25	2.75	3.25	3.5	3.75	4.25	5	5.5	6	6.5	9.0

Blu-- N--t--

designed by Sandy Scoville

Size:
About 40" x 50"

Materials:
Worsted weight yarn, 20 oz (1400 yds, 560 gms)
off white; 15 oz (1050 yds, 420 gms) blue
Size 9 (5.25mm) 29" circular knitting needle, or size
required for gauge
Cable needle

Gauge:
9 sts = 2" in stockinette st (knit one row, purl
one row)

7 patt repeats = 6"

Pattern Stitches

Cable Left (CL):
* Sl next st to cable needle, hold in front of work;
K2, K1 from cable needle—CL made.

Cable Right (CR):
Sl next 2 sts to cable needle, hold in back of work;
K1, K2 from cable needle—CR made.

Instructions

Center
Note: Carry unused yarn along side edge. Slip all sts
as to purl.

With off white, cast on 149 sts.

Row 1 (right side):
K1; * sl 1, K3; rep from * 36 times more.

Row 2:
P3, sl 1; rep from * 36 times more; P1.

Row 3:
With blue, K1; * CL (see Pattern Stitches); K1; rep
from * 36 times more.

Row 4:
Purl.

Row 5:
With off white, K5; * sl 1, K3; rep from * 35 times
more.

Row 6:
* P3, sl 1; rep from * 35 times more; P5.

Row 7:
With blue, K3; * CR (see Pattern Stitches); K1; rep
from * 35 times more; K2.

Row 8:
Purl.

Rep Rows 1 through 8 until center measures about
48", ending by working a Row 8. Cut blue.

Next Row:
With off white, rep Row 1.
Bind off.

Side Border (make 2)
Note: Slip all sts as to purl.

With off white, cast on 17 sts.

Row 1 (right side):
K1, YO, sl 1, K1, PSSO; K1, K2 tog; YO, K7, YO,
K2 tog; K2.

Row 2:
P3, YO, P2 tog; P12.

Row 3:
K1, YO, K2 tog; YO, K3, YO, sl 1, K1, PSSO; K5, YO,
K2 tog; K2—18 sts.

Row 4:
P3, YO, P2 tog; P13.

Row 5:
K1, YO, K2 tog; YO, K5, YO, sl 1, K1, PSSO; K4, YO, K2 tog; K2—19 sts.

Row 6:
P3, YO, P2 tog; P14.

Row 7:
K1, YO, K2 tog; YO, K3, YO, sl 1, K1, PSSO; K2, YO, sl 1, K1, PSSO; K3, YO, K2 tog; K2—20 sts.

Row 8:
P3, YO, P2 tog; P15.

Row 9:
K1, YO, K2 tog; YO, K3, (YO, sl 1, K1, PSSO) twice; K2, YO, sl 1, K1, PSSO; K2, YO, K2 tog; K2—21 sts.

Rnd 10:
P3, YO, P2 tog; P16.

Row 11:
K1, YO, K2 tog; YO, K3, (YO, sl 1, K1, PSSO) 3 times; K2, YO, sl 1, K1, PSSO; K1, YO, K2 tog; K2—22 sts.

Row 12:
P3, YO, P2 tog; P17.

Row 13:
Sl 1, K1, PSSO; (YO, sl 1, K1, PSSO) twice; K2, (YO, sl 1, K1, PSSO) twice; K1, K2 tog; YO, K3, YO, K2 tog; K2—21 sts.

Row 14:
P3, YO, P2 tog; P16.

Row 15:
Sl 1, K1, PSSO; (YO, sl 1, K1, PSSO) twice; K2, YO, sl 1, K1, PSSO; K1, K2 tog; YO, K4, YO, K2 tog; K2—20 sts.

Row 16:
P3, YO, P2 tog; P15.

Row 17:
Sl 1, K1, PSSO; (YO, sl 1, K1, PSSO) twice; K3, K2 tog; YO, K5, YO, K2 tog; K2—19 sts.

Row 18:
P3, YO, P2 tog; P14.

Row 19:
Sl 1, K1, PSSO; (YO, sl 1, K1, PSSO) twice; K1, K2 tog; YO, K6, YO, K2 tog; K2—18 sts.

Row 20:
P3, YO, P2 tog; P13.

Row 21:
Sl 1, K1, PSSO; YO, sl 1, K1, PSSO; K1, K2 tog; YO, K7, YO, K2 tog; K2—17 sts.

Row 22:
P3, YO, P2 tog; P12.

Rep Rows 3 through 22 until border measures about 49". Bind off.

Assembly

Cut 2 strands of blue about 60" long. With tapestry needle, weave strands in and out of eyelets made by YOs along straight edge of border. Secure ends.

Hold one border piece and right-hand edge of center piece with right sides together. With tapestry needle and off white, sew together.

Turn second border piece upside down; hold border piece and left-hand edge of center piece with right sides together. With tapestry needle and off white, sew together.

Top and Lower Borders

Hold throw with right side facing you and cast-on edge at top. With off white, pick up 183 sts across borders and center.

Knit 5 rows.

Bind off.

Work top border in same manner.

Twi ti.. .-.-.-l

designed by Kathy Wesley

Size:
About 42" x 52"

Materials:
Worsted weight yarn, 35 oz (2450 yds, 1000 gms)
  pink
Size 10 (5.75mm) 29" circular knitting needle, or size
  required for gauge

Gauge:
4 sts = 1" in stockinette st (knit one row, purl
  one row)
6 rows = 1"

Special Abbreviation

Slip, Slip, Knit (SSK):
Sl next 2 sts, one at a time, as to knit; insert left-
hand needle through both sts from right to left;
K2 tog—SSK made.

Pattern Stitch

Cable Front (CF):
Slip next 3 sts onto cable needle and hold in front
of work, K4, K3 sts from cable needle—CF made.

Instructions

Lower Border
Cast on 197 sts.

Row 1 (right side):
Knit.

Row 2:
Knit.

Row 3:
K1, P1, K1 tbl; * P4, K7, P4, K1 tbl; rep from * 11
times more; P1, K1.

Row 4:
K2, P1 tbl; * K4, P7, K4, P1 tbl; rep from * 11 times
more; K2.

Row 5:
K1, P1, knit in front, in back, and in front of next st;
* P4, K7, P4, knit in front, in back, and in front of next
st; rep from * 11 times more; P1, K1.

Row 6:
K2, P3 tog; * K4, P7, K4, P3 tog; rep from * 11 times
more; K2.

Rows 7 through 10:
Rep Rows 3 through 6.

Body
Row 1:
K1, P1, K1 tbl, P4; * CF (see Pattern Stitch); P4, K1 tbl,
P4; rep from * 10 times more; CF; P4, K1 tbl, P1, K1.

Row 2:
K2, P1 tbl, K4; * P7, K4, P1 tbl, K4; rep from * 10
times more; P7, K4, P1 tbl, K2.

Row 3:
K1, P1, knit in front, in back, and in front of next st;
P4; * † K2 tog; YO, K1, P1, K1, YO, SSK (see Special
Abbreviation); P4, knit in front, in back, and in front
of next st †; P4; rep from * 10 times more, then rep
from † to † once; P1, K1.

Row 4:
K2, P3 tog; K4; * P7, K4, P3 tog; K4; rep from * 10
times more; P7, K4, P3 tog; K2.

Row 5:
K1, P1, K1 tbl, P4; * K3, P1, K3, P4, K1 tbl, P4; rep
from * 10 times more; K3, P1, K3, P4, K1 tbl, P1, K1.

Row 6:
K2, P1 tbl, K4; * P7, K4, P1 tbl, K4; rep from * 10 times more; P7, K4, P1 tbl, K2.

Rows 7 through 18:
Rep Rows 3 through 6 three times more.

Row 19:
K1, P1, knit in front, in back, and in front of next st; P4; * CF; P4, knit in front, in back, and in front of next st; P4; rep from * 10 times more; CF; P4, knit in front, in back, and in front of next st; P1, K1.

Row 20:
K2, P3 tog, K4; * P7, K4, P3 tog; K4; rep from * 10 times more; P7, K4, P3 tog; K2.

Row 21:
K1, P1, K1 tbl, P4; * K7, P4, K1 tbl, P4; rep from * 10 times more; K7, P4, K1 tbl, P1, K1.

Row 22:
K2, P1 tbl, K4; * P7, K4, P1 tbl, K4; rep from * 10 times more; P7, K4, P1 tbl, K2.

Row 23:
K1, P1, knit in front, in back, and in front of next st; P4; * K7, P4, knit in front, in back, and in front of next st; P4; rep from * 10 times more; K7, P4, knit in front, in back, and in front of next st; P1, K1.

Row 24:
K2, P3 tog; K4; * P7, K4, P3 tog; K4; rep from * 10 times more; P7, K4, P3 tog; K2.

Row 25:
K1, P1, K1 tbl, P4; * CF; P4, K1 tbl, P4; rep from * 10 times more; CF; P4, K1 tbl, P1, K1.

Row 26:
K2, P1 tbl, K4; * P7, K4, P1 tbl, K4; rep from * 10 times more; P7, K4, P1 tbl, K2.

Rep Rows 3 through 26 until piece measures about 45" from cast-on edge.

Rep Rows 3 through 20.

Upper Border:
Rep Rows 3 through 6 of lower border twice.

Next Row:
Knit.

Bind off.

Fringe
Following Fringe instructions on page 8, make Double Knot fringe. Cut 30" strands of yarn; use 8 strands for each knot. Tie knots evenly spaced (about every 5 sts) across each short end of afghan. Trim ends even.

Classic Diamonds

designed by Kathy Wesley

Size:
About 42" x 52"

Materials:
Worsted weight yarn, 30 oz (1500 yds,
    840 gms) green
Size 10 (5.75mm) circular knitting needle, or size
    required for gauge

Gauge:
4 sts = 1" in stockinette st (knit one row, purl
    one row)
5 rows = 1"

Special Abbreviation

Slip, Slip, Knit (SSK):
Sl next 2 sts, one at a time, as to knit; insert left-
hand needle through both sts from right to left;
K2 tog—SSK made.

Instructions
Cast on 153 sts.

Lower Border

Row 1 (wrong side):
K1, purl to last st; K1.

Row 2 (right side):
K2; * K2 tog; YO, K1, YO, SSK (see Special
Abbreviation); K1; rep from * 24 times more; K1.

Rows 3 through 10:
Rep Rows 1 and 2 four times more.

Row 11:
Rep Row 1.

Body

Row 1 (right side):
K2, K2 tog; YO, K1, YO, SSK; K1; * K6, (YO, SSK) 3
times; K6, K2 tog; YO, K1, YO, SSK; K1; rep from * 5
times more; K1.

Row 2 and all even numbered rows:
K1, purl to last st; K1.

Row 3:
K2, K2 tog; YO, K1, YO, SSK; K1; * K4, K2 tog; YO,
K1, (YO, SSK) 3 times; K5, K2 tog; YO, K1, YO, SSK;
K1; rep from * 5 times more; K1.

Row 5:
K2, K2 tog; YO, K1, YO, SSK; K1; * K3, (K2 tog, YO)
twice; K1, (YO, SSK) 3 times; K4, K2 tog; YO, K1, YO,
SSK; K1; rep from * 5 times more; K1.

Row 7:
K2, K2 tog; YO, K1, YO, SSK; K1; * K2, (K2 tog, YO) 3
times; K1, (YO, SSK) 3 times; K3, K2 tog; YO, K1, YO,
SSK; K1; rep from * 5 times more; K1.

Row 9:
K2, K2 tog; YO, K1, YO, SSK; K1; * K1, (K2 tog, YO) 3
times; K3, (YO, SSK) 3 times; K2, K2 tog; YO, K1, YO,
SSK; K1; rep from * 5 times more; K1.

Row 11:
K2, K2 tog; YO, K1, YO, SSK; K1; * (K2 tog, YO) 3
times; K5, (YO, SSK) 3 times; K1, K2 tog; YO, K1, YO,
SSK; K1; rep from * 5 times more; K1.

Row 13:
K2, K2 tog; YO, K1, YO, SSK; K1; * (YO, SSK) twice; YO, K3, sl 1 as to knit, K2 tog, PSSO; K3, (YO, K2 tog) twice; YO, K1, K2 tog; YO, K1, YO, SSK; K1; rep from * 5 times more; K1.

Row 15:
K2, K2 tog; YO, K1, YO, SSK; K1; * K1, (YO, SSK) twice; YO, K2, sl 1 as to knit, K2 tog, PSSO; K2, (YO, K2 tog) twice; YO, K2, K2 tog; YO, K1, YO, SSK; K1; rep from * 5 times more; K1.

Row 17:
K2, K2 tog; YO, K1, YO, SSK; K1; * K2, (YO, SSK) twice; YO, K1, sl 1 as to knit, K2 tog, PSSO; K1, (YO, K2 tog) twice; YO, K3, K2 tog; YO, K1, YO, SSK; K1; rep from * 5 times more; K1.

Row 19:
K2, K2 tog; YO, K1, YO, SSK; K1; * K3, (YO, SSK) twice; YO, sl 1 as to knit, K2 tog; PSSO; (YO, K2 tog) twice; YO, K4, K2 tog; YO, K1, YO, SSK; K1; rep from * 5 times more; K1.

Row 21:
K2, K2 tog; YO, K1, YO, SSK; K1; * K4, (YO, SSK) twice; YO, sl 1 as to knit, K2 tog; PSSO; YO, K2 tog; YO, K5, K2 tog; YO, K1, YO, SSK, K1; rep from * 5 times more; K1.

Row 23:
K2, K2 tog; YO, K1, YO, SSK; K1; * K5, (YO, SSK) twice; YO, sl 1 as to knit, K2 tog, PSSO; YO, K6, K2 tog; YO, K1, YO, SSK; K1; rep from * 5 times more; K1.

Row 24:
K1, purl to last st; K1.

Rep Rows 1 through 24 until piece measures about 50" from cast-on edge.

Rep Rows 1 and 2 once more.

Upper Border:

Row 1 (right side)**:**
K2; * K2 tog; YO, K1, YO, SSK; K1; rep from * 24 times more; K1.

Row 2:
K1, purl to last st; K1.

Rows 3 through 10:
Rep Rows 1 and 2 four times more.

Bind off.

Fringe
Following Fringe instructions on page 8, make Spagetti Knot fringe. Cut 25" strands. Tie knots in every st across each short end of afghan. Trim ends even.

designed by Sandy Scoville

Size:
About 40" x 50"

Materials:
Worsted weight yarn, 30 oz (2100 yds, 850 gms)
   green; 18 oz (1260 yds, 510 gms) off white
Size 9 (5.25mm) 29" circular knitting needle, or size
   required for gauge
Cable needle
Size H (5mm) crochet hook (optional for
   side edgings)

Gauge:
9 sts = 2" in stockinette st (knit one row, purl
   one row)
6 patt repeats = 10"

Instructions
Note: Carry unused yarn along side edge. Slip all sts
as to purl. Carry yarn loosely behind slipped sts on
purl side.

With off white, cast on 172 sts.

Row 1 (right side):
Purl.

Rows 2 and 3:
Knit.

Row 4:
With green, P1, sl 2; * P6, sl 2; rep from * 20 times
more; P1.

Row 5:
K1, sl 2; * K6, sl 2; rep from * 20 times more; K1.

Rows 6 through 9:
Rep Rows 4 and 5 twice more.

Rows 10 and 11:
With off white, purl.

Rows 12 and 13:
Knit.

Row 14:
With green, P5, sl 2; * P6, sl 2; rep from * 19 times
more; P5.

Row 15:
K5, sl 2; * K6, sl 2; rep from * 19 times more; K5.

Rows 16 through 19:
Rep Rows 14 and 15 twice more.

Rows 20 and 21:
With off white, purl.

Rows 22 and 23:
Knit.

Rep Rows 4 through 23 until piece measures about
50" long, ending last rep by working a Row 21.
Bind off.

Side Edgings (optional)

Note: See Special Techniques beginning on page 5 for instructions on working single crochet stitches.

Hold afghan with right side facing you and one side edge at top; make loop on hook and join with a single crochet stitch in side of first row in right-hand corner. Work one row of single crochet stitches along side edge, spacing stitches so edges lay flat. At end of row, ch 1, turn. Work second row of single crochet stitches across previous row. At end of row, finish off. Repeat edging along remaining side edge. Weave in all ends.

Tassels (make 44)

Cut 5" long piece of cardboard. For each tassel, wind off white 31 times around cardboard; cut once through all strands. Tie one stand tightly around 30 strands at center, leaving ends of tie to attach to afghan. Fold strands in half over tie; wrap green yarn around strands several times to form tassel. Attach 22 tassels evenly spaced across each short end of afghan. Trim ends even.

Blue Tile

designed by Nicky Epstein, design courtesy of The NeedleWorks

Size:
About 42" x 54"

Materials:
Worsted weight yarn, 28 oz (1864 yds, 800 gms) off white; 3½ oz (233 yds, 10 gms) each royal blue, blue, and baby blue

Size 8 (5mm) 29" circular knitting needle, or size required for gauge

Gauge:
9 sts = 2" in stockinette st (knit one row, purl one row)

24 rows = 4"

Instructions
Note: Slip sts as to purl. Tile motifs are worked in duplicate st after afghan is knitted.

With off white, cast on 185 sts.

Row 1 (right side):
K1; * YO, K2, sl 1, K2 tog, PSSO; K2, YO, K1; rep from * 22 times more.

Row 2 and all even numbered rows:
Purl.

Row 3:
K2; * YO, K1, sl 1, K2 tog, PSSO; K1, YO, K3; rep from * 21 times more; YO, K1, sl 1, K2 tog, PSSO; K1, YO, K2.

Row 5:
K3; * YO, sl 1, K2 tog, PSSO; YO, K5; rep from * 21 times more; YO, sl 1, K2 tog, PSSO; YO, K3.

Rows 7 through 12:
Rep Rows 1 through 6.

Row 13:
✝ K1, YO, K2, sl 1, K2 tog, PSSO; K2, YO, K1 ✝; K35; * K2 tog; K2, YO, K1, YO, K2, K2 tog tbl; K35; rep from * twice more, then rep from ✝ to ✝ once.

Row 15:
✝ K2, YO, K1, sl 1, K2 tog, PSSO; K1, YO, K2 ✝; K35; * K2 tog; K1, YO, K3, YO, K1, K2 tog tbl; K35; rep from * twice more, then rep from ✝ to ✝ once.

Row 17:
✝ K3, YO, sl 1, K2 tog, PSSO; YO, K3 ✝; K35; * K2 tog; YO, K5, YO, K2 tog tbl; K35; rep from * once more, then rep from ✝ to ✝ once.

Rows 19 through 60:
Rep Rows 13 through 18 seven times more.

Rows 61 through 300:
Rep Rows 1 through 60 four times more.

Rows 301 through 311:
Rep Rows 1 through 11 once.

Bind off.

With tapestry needle and blue yarn, work duplicate st (see Special Techniques on page 7) on right side of afghan, following charts and placement diagram.

Key

☐	– off white
■	– royal blue
○	– blue
—	– pale blue

Chart Placement Diagram

3	1	2	1
1	2	1	3
2	1	3	1
1	3	1	2
3	1	2	1

Note: Numbers refer to chart numbers.

Chart 1 (continue pattern for entire square—48 rows)

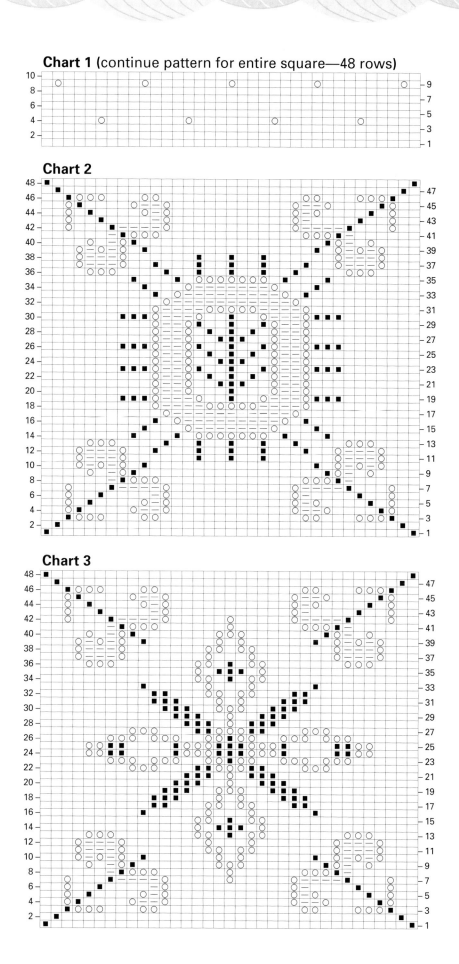

Chart 2

Chart 3

Celtic Knot

designed by Maureen Egan Emlet, design courtesy of The NeedleWorks

Size:
About 58" x 64"

Materials:
Worsted weight yarn, 52½ oz (3600 yds, 1500 gms) grey
Size 9 (5.25mm) 29" circular knitting needle, or size required for gauge
Cable needle
Markers
Size 16 tapestry needle

Gauge:
20 sts = 4" in patt
24 patt rows = 4"

Pattern Stitches

Popcorn (PC):
In next st work (K1, YO) twice; K1 in same st; turn, P5, turn, K5, turn, P2 tog; P1, P2 tog; turn, sl 1, K2 tog, PSSO—PC made.

Cable Front (CF):
Sl next 2 sts onto cable needle and hold in front of work; K2, K2 from cable needle—CF made.

Cable Back (CB):
Sl next 2 sts onto cable needle and hold in back of work; K2, K2 from cable needle—CB made.

Twist Three Front (T3F):
Sl next 2 sts onto cable needle and hold in front of work; P1, K2 from cable needle—T3F made.

Twist Three Back (T3B):
Sl next st onto cable needle and hold in back of work; K2, P1 from cable needle—T3B made.

Twist Four Front (T4F):
Sl next 2 sts onto cable needle and hold in front of work; P2, K2 from cable needle—T4F made.

Twist Four Back (T4B):
Sl next 2 sts onto cable needle and hold in back of work; K2, P2 from cable needle—T4B made.

Twist Five Front (T5F):
Sl next 2 sts onto cable needle and hold in front of work; P3, K2 from cable needle—T5F made.

Twist Five Back (T5B):
Sl next 3 sts onto cable needle and hold in back of work; K2, P3 from cable needle—T5B made.

Decrease (dec):
P2 tog; P3 tog tbl; pass P2 tog st over P3 tog tbl—dec made.

Special Abbreviations

SK2P:
Sl 1 as to knit, K2 tog, PSSO.

SSK:
Sl next 2 sts as to knit, one at a time; insert left-hand needle from left to right into fronts of these 2 sts; K2 tog.

M1 (make 1):
With left-hand needle, lift strand between last st worked and next st on left-hand needle, purl.

Instructions

Note: When working a YO after a knit stitch and before a purl stitch, bring yarn forward, completely around the needle, and forward again to complete the stitch.

Loosely cast on 272 sts.

Border Pattern

Row 1 (right side):
* K1, P1; rep from * across.

Row 2:
Knit.

Rows 3 through 16:
Rep Rows 1 and 2 seven times more.

Row 17:
(K1, P1) 6 times; * PC (see Pattern Stitches); (P1, K1) 6 times; PC; (K1, P1) 6 times; rep from * 9 times more—20 PC.

Row 18:
Rep Row 2.

Rows 19 through 28:
Rep Rows 1 and 2 five times.

Row 29:
Rep Row 1.

Row 30:
K25; place marker; * K9, inc (knit in front and back of next st); rep from * 21 times more; K2; place marker; K25—294 sts.

Body:

Note: Slip markers as you come to them.

Row 1:
K1, (P1, K1) 12 times; * † YO, SSK (see Special Abbreviations); K1, K2 tog; YO, P5, K4, P5, YO, SSK; K1, K2 tog; YO †; P8, K4, P8; rep from * 4 times more, then rep from † to † once; P1, (K1, P1) 12 times.

Row 2:
K25; * † P5, K5, P4, K5, P5 †; K8, P4, K8; rep from * 4 times more, then rep from † to † once; K25.

Note: At end of Row 3—334 sts; 284 sts between markers.

Row 3:
K1, (P1, K1) 12 times; * † K1, YO, SK2P (see Special Abbreviations); YO, K1, P5, CB (see Pattern Stitches); P5, K1, YO, SK2P; YO, K1 †; P2, M1 (see Special Abbreviations); double increase (to work double inc: knit in front and back and front of next st—double increase made); M1, P3, T4B (see Pattern Stitches); T4F (see Pattern Stitches); P3, M1, double increase; M1, P2; rep from * 4 times more, then rep from † to † once; P1, (K1, P1) 12 times.

Row 4:
K25; * † P5, K5, P4, K5, P5 †; K2, P2, K1, P2, K3, P2, K4, P2, K3, P2, K1, P2, K2; rep from * 4 times more, then rep from † to † once; K25.

Row 5:
K1, (P1, K1) 12 times; * † YO, SSK; K1, K2 tog; YO, P5, K4, P5, YO, SSK; K1, K2 tog; YO †; P1, T3B (see Pattern Stitches); P1, T4F; T3B; P4, T3F (see Pattern Stitches); T4B; P1, T3F; P1; rep from * 4 times more, then rep from † to † once; P1, (K1, P1) 12 times.

Row 6:
K25; * † P5, K5, P4, K5, P5 †; K1, P2, K4, P4, K6, P4, K4, P2, K1; rep from * 4 times more, then rep from † to † once; K25.

Row 7:
K1, (P1, K1) 12 times; * † K1, YO, SK2P; YO, K1, P5, CB; P5, K1, YO, SK2P; YO, K1 †; T3B; P4, CF (see Pattern Stitches); P6, CF; P4, T3F; rep from * 4 times more, then rep from † to † once; P1, (K1, P1) 12 times.

Row 8:
K25; * † P5, K5, P4, K5, P5 †; P2, K5, P4, K6, P4, K5, P2; rep from * 4 times more, then rep from † to † once; K25.

Row 9:
K1, (P1, K1) 12 times; * † YO, SSK; K1, K2 tog; YO, P5, K4, P5, YO, SSK; K1, K2 tog; YO †; K2, P4, T3B; T5F (see Pattern Stitches); T5B (see Pattern Stitches); T3F; P4, K2; rep from * 4 times more, then rep from † to † once; P1, (K1, P1) 12 times.

continued

Row 10:
K25; * † P5, K5, P4, K5, P5 †; (P2, K4) twice; P4, (K4, P2) twice; rep from * 4 times more, then rep from † to † once; K25.

Row 11:
K1, (P1, K1) 12 times; * † K1, YO, SK2P; YO, K1, P3, T4B; T4F; P3, K1, YO, SK2P; YO, K1 †; T3F; P2, T3B; P4, CB; P4, T3F; P2, T3B; rep from * 4 times more, then rep from † to † once; P1, (K1, P1) 12 times.

Row 12:
K25; * † P5, K3, P2, K4, P2, K3, P5 †; K1, P2, K2, P2, K5, P4, K5, P2, K2, P2, K1; rep from * 4 times more, then rep from † to † once; K25.

Row 13:
K1, (P1, K1) 12 times; * † YO, SSK; K1, K2 tog; YO, P1, T4B; (K1, P1) twice; T4F; P1, YO, SSK; K1, K2 tog; YO †; P1, T3F; T3B; P5, K4, P5, T3F; T3B; P1; rep from * 4 times more, then rep from † to † once; P1, (K1, P1) 12 times.

Row 14:
K25; * † P5, K1, P2, K8, P2, K1, P5 †; K2, P4, (K6, P4) twice; K2; rep from * 4 times more, then rep from † to † once; K25.

Row 15:
K1, (P1, K1) 12 times; * † K1, YO, SK2P; YO, K1, T3B; (K1, P1) 4 times; T3F; K1, YO, SK2P; YO, K1 †; P2, (CB, P6) twice; CB; P2; rep from * 4 times more, then rep from † to † once; P1, (K1, P1) 12 times.

Row 16:
K25; * † P7, K10, P7 †; K2, P4, (K6, P4) twice; K2; rep from * 4 times more, then rep from † to † once; K25.

Row 17:
(K1, P1) 6 times; PC; (P1, K1) 6 times; * † YO, SSK; K1, K2 tog; YO, K2, (P1, K1) 5 times; K2, YO, SSK; K1, K2 tog; YO †; P1, T3B; T3F; P5, K4, P5, T3B; T3F; P1; rep from * 4 times more, then rep from † to † once; (P1, K1) 6 times; PC; (K1, P1) 6 times.

Row 18:
K25; * † P7, K10, P7 †; K1, P2, K2, P2, K5, P4, K5, P2, K2, P2, K1; rep from * 4 times more, then rep from † to † once; K25.

Row 19:
K1, (P1, K1) 12 times; * † K1, YO, SK2P; YO, K3, (P1, K1) 5 times; K3, YO, SK2P; YO, K1 †; T3B; P2, T3F; P4, CB; P4, T3B; P2, T3F; rep from * 4 times more, then rep from † to † once; P1, (K1, P1) 12 times.

Row 20:
K25; * † P7, K10, P7 †; (P2, K4) twice; P4, (K4, P2) twice; rep from * 4 times more, then rep from † to † once; K25.

Row 21:
K1, (P1, K1) 12 times; * † YO, SSK; K1, K2 tog; YO, T3F; (K1, P1) 4 times; T3B; YO, SSK; K1, K2 tog; YO †; K2, P4, T3F; T5B; T5F; T3B; P4, K2; rep from * 4 times more, then rep from † to † once; P1, (K1, P1) 12 times.

Row 22:
K25; * † P5, K1, P2, K8, P2, K1, P5 †; P2, K5, P4, K6, P4, K5, P2; rep from * 4 times more, then rep from † to † once; K25.

Row 23:
K1, (P1, K1) 12 times; * † K1, YO, SK2P; YO, K1, P1, T4F; (K1, P1) twice; T4B; P1, K1, YO, SK2P; YO, K1 †; T3F; P4, CF; P6, CF; P4, T3B; rep from * 4 times more, then rep from † to † once; P1, (K1, P1) 12 times.

Row 24:
K25; * † P5, K3, P2, K4, P2, K3, P5 †; K1, P2, K4, P4, K6, P4, K4, P2, K1; rep from * 4 times more, then rep from † to † once; K25.

Row 25:
K1, (P1, K1) 12 times; * † YO, SSK, K1, K2 tog; YO, P3, T4F; T4B; P3, YO, SSK, K1, K2 tog; YO †; P1, T3F; P1, T4B; T3F; P4, T3B; T4F; P1, T3B; P1; rep from * 4 times more, then rep from † to † once; P1, (K1, P1) 12 times.

Note: At the end of Row 26—294 sts; 244 sts between markers.

Row 26:
K25; * † P5, K5, P4, K5, P5 †; K2, dec (see Pattern Stitches); K3, P2, K4, P2, K3, 5-to-1 dec; K2; rep from * 4 times more, then rep from † to † once; K25.

Row 27:
K1 (P1, K1) 12 times; * † K1, YO, SK2P; YO, K1, P5, K4, P5, K1, YO, SK2P; YO, K1 †; P6, T4F; T4B; P6; rep from * 4 times more, then rep from † to † once; P1, (K1, P1) 12 times.

Row 28:
K25; * † P5, K5, P4, K5, P5 †; K8, P4, K8; rep from * 4 times more, then rep from † to † once; K25.

Row 29:
K1, (P1, K1) 12 times; * † YO, SSK; K1, K2 tog; YO, P5, CB; P5, YO, SSK; K1, K2 tog; YO †; P8, CB; P8; rep from * 4 times more, then rep from † to † once; P1, (K1, P1) 12 times.

Row 30:
K25; * † P5, K5, P4, K5, P5 †; K8, P4, K8; rep from * 4 times more, then rep from † to † once; K25.

Rows 31 through 330:
Rep Rows 1 through 30 of body ten times more.

Ending Border:
Row 1:
Work Row 1 of border patt, dec 22 sts evenly spaced between markers.

Rows 2 through 30:
Rep Rows 2 through 30 of border patt.

Bind off.

Weave in all ends.

Finishing
Hold afghan with right side facing you; fold first 2 sts along one side edge toward the wrong side. With tapestry needle and yarn, sew in place to form hem. Repeat for hem along other side edge.

American Beauty Rose

adapted by Sandy Scoville

Size:
About 40" x 50"

Materials:
Worsted weight yarn, 8 oz (560 yds, 280 gms) each lt blue and med blue; 12 oz (840 yds, 420 gms) each blue ombre and off white; 11 oz (770 yds, 365 gms) rose

Size 10½ (6.5mm) 29" circular knitting needle, or size required for gauge

Gauge:
7 sts = 2" in stockinette st (knit one row, purl one row)

Instructions
With lt blue, cast on 179 sts.

Row 1 (right side):
Knit.

Row 2:
Knit.

Row 3:
K5; * K1, YO, K4, sl 1 as to knit, K2 tog, PSSO; K4, YO, K1; rep from * 12 times more; K5.

Row 4:
K5, purl to last 5 sts; K5.

Rows 5 and 6:
Rep Rows 3 and 4.

Rows 7 through 210:
Rep Rows 3 and 4 in following color sequence:

2 rows rose

8 rows blue ombre

2 rows rose

6 rows med blue

4 rows rose

8 rows off white

6 rows lt blue

2 rows rose

8 rows blue ombre

2 rows rose

6 rows med blue

4 rows rose

8 rows off white

6 rows lt blue

2 rows rose

8 rows blue ombre

2 rows rose

6 rows med blue

4 rows rose

8 rows off white

4 rows rose

6 rows dk blue

2 rows rose

8 rows blue ombre

2 rows rose

6 rows lt blue

8 rows off white

4 rows rose

6 rows med blue

2 rows rose

8 rows blue ombre

2 rows rose

6 rows lt blue

8 rows off white

4 rows rose

6 rows med blue

2 rows rose

8 rows blue ombre

2 rows rose

4 rows lt blue

With lt blue, knit 3 rows.

Bind off.

American Beauty Rose
page 24

Bobbles on Points
page 54

25

Cozy Elegance
page 48

Americana
page 42

Lodge Pillow & Afghan
page 50

Starlight
page 56

Twisting Cables
page 12

Celtic Knot
page 20

Blue Tile
page 18

Lazy Ribbing & Holly
page 44

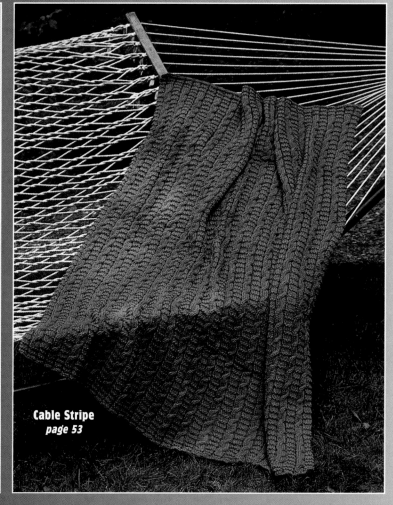

Cable Stripe
page 53

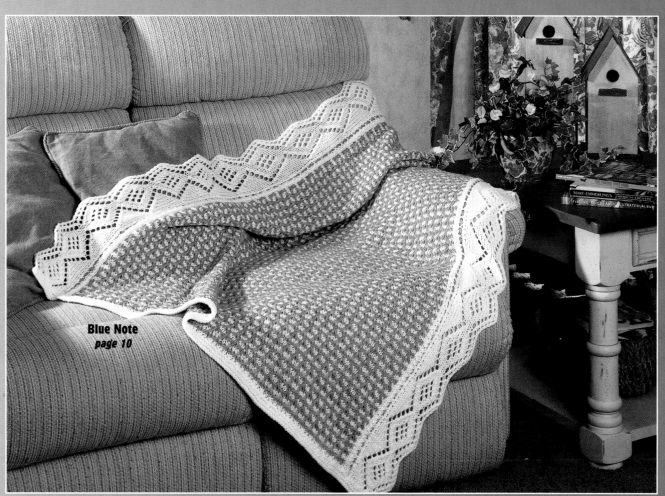

Blue Note
page 10

Classic Diamonds
page 14

Daffodil Dream
page 41

**Honeycomb
in the Garden**
page 16

Fisherman
page 36

Enchantment
page 35

Quick Knit
page 33

Peach Mist
page 40

Quick Knit

designed by Maureen Elena Malo, design courtesy of The NeedleWorks

Size:
About 48" x 60"

Materials:
Sport weight yarn, 48 oz (5760 yds, 1370 gms) rose;
  16 oz (1920 yds, 480 gms) pastel ombre; 4 oz
  (480 yds, 115 gms) each, turquoise, white,
  and lavender
Size 35 (19mm) 47" circular knitting needle, or size
  required for gauge
Size 15 (10mm) 29" circular knitting needle
Size 16 tapestry needle

Gauge:
With larger size needles and 8 strands held together:
7 sts = 5" in garter st (knit every row)
10 rows = 4"

Instructions

Center Panel
With 8 strands of rose held tog, loosely cast on 43 sts.

Row 1 (right side):
Knit.

Rep Row 1 until piece measures about 46" from cast-on edge, ending by working a wrong-side row. Do not bind off. Cut rose.

Top Border
Row 1 (right side):
With smaller size needle and 4 strands of ombre held tog, cast on one st; inc (knit in front and back of next st) in every st on center panel; cast on 1 st (see **Figs 1** and **2**)—88 sts.

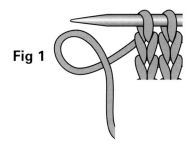

Fig 1

Fig 2

Row 2:
P2, K84, P2.

Row 3:
With turquoise, K2, inc; knit to last 3 sts; inc; K2—90 sts.

Row 4:
P2, knit to last 2 sts; P2.

Rows 5 through 31:
Rep Rows 3 and 4 in following color sequence:

continued

2 rows ombre

2 rows white

2 rows ombre

2 rows lavender

2 rows ombre

2 rows turquoise

2 rows ombre

2 rows white

2 rows ombre

2 rows lavender

2 rows ombre

2 rows turquoise

2 rows ombre

1 row white

With white, bind off loosely.

Lower Border

Row 1 (right side**):**

With smaller size needle and 4 strands of ombre held tog, cast on one st; pick up 2 sts in each cast-on st on center panel; cast on one st—88 sts.

Rows 2 through through 31:

Rep Rows 2 through 31 of top border.

With white, bind off loosely.

Side Borders

Hold center panel with right side facing you and one side edge at top; with smaller size needle and 4 strands of ombre held tog, pick up 105 sts evenly spaced along side edge.

Rep Rows 2 through 31 of top border.

With white, bind off loosely.

Work other side border in same manner.

Sew corner seams.

nchatment

designed by Sandy Scoville

Size:
About 40" x 52"

Materials:
Bulky weight brushed yarn, 18 oz (630 yds, 504 gms)
   each violet and variegated
Size 17 (12mm) 47" circular knitting needle, or size
   required for gauge

Gauge:
8 sts = 4" in stockinette st (knit one row, purl one
row)

Pattern Stitch

Cluster (CL):
P3 tog leaving sts on left-hand needle; YO, purl
same 3 sts tog—CL made.

Instructions
Note: Carry unused color along side edge, twisting
every other row.

With violet, loosely cast on 103 sts.

Row 1 (right side):
With violet, knit.

Row 2:
With violet, K1, P1; * CL (see Pattern Stitch); P1; rep
from * 24 times more; K1.

Row 3:
With variegated, knit.

Row 4:
With variegated, K1, P3, CL; * P1, CL; rep from * 22
times more; P3, K1.

Rep Rows 1 through 4 until piece measures
about 51".

Next Row:
With violet, knit.
Bind off loosely.

Fringe
Following Fringe instructions on page 8, with violet,
make Single Knot fringe. Cut 25" strands of yarn; use
6 strands for each knot. Tie knots evenly spaced
across each short end of afghan. Trim ends even.

isherman

designed by Rita Weiss

Size:
About 41" x 53"

Materials:
Worsted weight yarn, 40 oz (2325 yds, 1175 gms)
  off white
Size 9 (5.25mm) 29" circular knitting needle
Cable Needle
Size 16 tapestry needle

Pattern Stitches

Cable Back (CB):
Sl next 2 sts onto cable needle and hold in back of work, K2, K2 from cable needle—CB made.

Cable Front (CF):
Sl next 2 sts onto cable needle and hold in front of work, K2, K2 from cable needle—CF made.

Twist Left (TL):
Sl next 2 sts onto cable needle and hold in front of work, P2, K2 from cable needle—TL made.

Twist Right (TR):
Sl next 2 sts onto cable needle and hold in back of work, K2, P2 from cable needle—TR made.

Popcorn (PC):
In next st work (P1, K1, P1, K1); slip 2nd, 3rd and 4th st on right-hand needle over first st—PC made.

Back Cross (BC):
Sl next st onto cable needle and hold in back of work, K2, P1 from cable needle—BC made.

Front Cross (FC):
Sl 2 sts onto cable needle and hold in front of work, P1, K2 from cable needle—FC made.

Instructions

Note: Afghan is worked in panels, then sewn together. Work each panel to same length. Slip all sts as to knit.

Panel A (make one)
Cast on 80 sts.

Row 1 (right side):
* P2, K4, P2, K2, P8, CB (see Pattern Stitches); P8, K2, P2, K4, P2; rep from * once more.

Row 2:
* K2, P4, K2, P2, K8, P4, K8, P2, K2, P4, K2; rep from * once more.

Row 3:
* P2, CF (see Pattern Stitches); P2; † TL (see Pattern Stitches); P4, TR (see Pattern Stitches) †; rep from † to † once more; P2, CB; P2; rep from * once more.

Row 4:
* K2, P4, K4, (P2, K4) 4 times; P4, K2; rep from * once more.

Row 5:
* P2, K4, P4, (TL, TR, P4) twice; K4, P2; rep from * once more.

Row 6:
* K2, P4, K6, P4, K8, P4, K6, P4, K2; rep from * once more.

Row 7:
* P2, K4, P6, CB; P3, [PC (see Pattern Stitches)] twice; P3, CB; P6, K4, P2; rep from * once more.

Row 8:
* K2, P4, K6, P4, K8, P4, K6, P4, K2; rep from * once more.

Row 9:
* P2, CF; P4, (TR, TL, P4) twice; CB; P2; rep from * once more.

Row 10:
* K2, P4, K4, (P2, K4) 4 times; P4, K2; rep from * once more.

Row 11:
* P2, K4, P2, (TR, P4, TL) twice; P2, K4, P2; rep from * once more.

Row 12:
* K2, P4, K2, P2, K8, P4, K8, P2, K2, P4, K2; rep from * once more.

Row 13:
* P2, K4, P2, K2, P3, PC twice; P3, CB; P3, PC twice; P3, K2, P2, K4, P2; rep from * once more.

Rows 14 through 301:
Rep Rows 2 through 13, 24 times more.

Rows 302 through 312:
Rep Rows 2 through 12 once.

Row 313:
* P2, K4, P2, K2, P8, CB; P8, K2, P2, K4, P2; rep from * once more.

Note: Panel should measure about 52" long.
Bind off.

Panel B (make 2)
Cast on 34 sts.

Row 1 (right side):
* P6, sl 2 sts onto cable needle and hold in front of work, K2, P1, K2 from cable needle; P6; rep from * once more.

Row 2:
* K6, P2, K1, P2, K6; rep from * once more.

Row 3:
* P5, BC (see Pattern Stitches); K1, FC (see Patten Stitches); P5; rep from * once more.

Row 4:
* K5, P2, K1, P1, K1, P2, K5; rep from * once more.

Row 5:
* P4, BC; K1, P1, K1, FC; P4; rep from * once more.

Row 6:
* K4, P2, (K1, P1) twice; K1, P2, K4; rep from * once more.

Row 7:
* P3, BC; (K1, P1) twice; K1, FC; P3; rep from * once more.

Row 8:
* K3, P2, (K1, P1) 3 times; K1, P2, K3; rep from * once more.

continued

Row 9:
* P2, BC; (K1, P1) 3 times; K1, FC; P2; rep from * once more.

Row 10:
* K2, P2, (K1, P1) 4 times; K1, P2, K2; rep from * once more.

Row 11:
* P1, BC; (K1, P1) 4 times; K1, FC; P1; rep from * once more.

Row 12:
* K1, P2, (K1, P1) 5 times; K1, P2, K1; rep from * once more.

Row 13:
* P1, FC; (P1, K1) 4 times; P1, BC; P1; rep from * once more.

Row 14:
* K2, P2, (K1, P1) 4 times; K1, P2, K2; rep from * once more.

Row 15:
* P2, FC; (P1, K1) 3 times; P1, BC; P2; rep from * once more.

Row 16:
* K3, P2, (K1, P1) 3 times; K1, P2, K3; rep from * once more.

Row 17:
* P3, FC; (P1, K1) twice; P1, BC; P3; rep from * once more.

Row 18:
* K4, P2, (K1, P1) twice; K1, P2, K4; rep from * once more.

Row 19:
* P4, FC; P1, K1, P1, BC; P4; rep from * once more.

Row 20:
* K5, P2, K1, P1, K1, P2, K5; rep from * once more.

Row 21:
* P5, FC; P1, BC; P5; rep from * once more.

Row 22:
* K6, P2, K1, P2, K6; rep from * once more.

Rows 23 through 308:
Rep Rows 1 through 22, 13 times more.

Row 309:
Rep Row 1.
Bind off.

Panel C (make 2)
Cast on 38 sts.

Row 1 (right side):
* K3, sl next st onto cable needle and hold in back of work, K1, K1 from cable needle, sl next st onto cable needle and hold in front of work, K1, K1 from cable needle; rep from * 4 times more; K3.

Row 2:
Purl.

Row 3:
P3; * sl next st onto cable needle and hold in front of work, K1, K1 from cable needle, sl next st onto cable needle and hold in back of work, K1, K1 from cable needle; P3; rep from * 4 times more.

Row 4:
Purl.

Rows 5 through 328:
Rep Rows 1 through 4 in sequence 81 times more.

Rows 329 through 331:
Rep Rows 1 through 3.
Bind off.

Assembly

Hold wrong side of one Panel C facing wrong side of one Panel B; sew panels together. Referring to **Diagram A**, sew remaining panels in same manner.

Diagram A

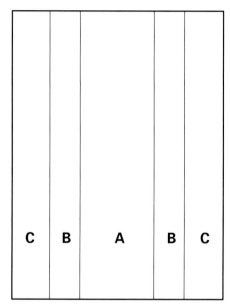

Note: If necessary, steam lightly. Do not touch iron to afghan.

Fringe

Following Fringe instructions on page 8, make Triple Knot fringe. Cut 30" strands of yarn; use 8 strands for each knot. Tie knots evenly spaced (about every 5 sts) across each short end of afghan. Trim ends even.

Beach Mit

designed by Rita Weiss

Size:
About 40" x 50"

Materials:
Bulky weight brushed yarn, 22½ oz (1035 yds, 638 gms) peach variegated

Size 10 (5.75mm) 29" circular needle, or size required for gauge

Gauge:
7 sts = 2" in stockinette st (knit one row, purl one row)

Instructions

Note: When dropping YOs, spread needles to separate strands.

Cast on 131 sts.

Row 1:
Knit.

Row 2:
Knit.

Row 3:
K5; * YO twice; K1, YO twice; K1, YO twice; K5; rep from * 17 times more.

Row 4:
K1; * K4, (drop YOs, K1) 3 times; rep from * 17 times more; K4.

Rows 5 and 6:
Knit.

Row 7:
K3, YO twice; * K5, (YO twice, K1) twice; YO twice; rep from * 17 times more; K2.

Row 8:
K2; * (drop YOs, K1) 3 times; K4; rep from * 17 times more; drop YOs, K3.

Rep Rows 1 through 8 until piece measures about 50", ending by working a Row 1.

Bind off loosely.

Fringe
Following Fringe instructions on page 8, make Spaghetti Knot fringe. Cut 25" strands of yarn. Tie knots in each st across each short end of afghan. Trim ends even.

Daffodil Dream

Size:
About 41" x 53"

Materials:
Worsted weight yarn, 21 oz (1470 yds,
    735 gms) yellow
Size 10½ (6.5mm) 29" circular knitting needle, or
    size required for gauge
Stitch markers

Gauge:
4 sts = 1" in stockinette st (knit one row, purl
    one row)

Instructions
Note: Slip markers as you come to them. Slip all sts
as to knit.

Cast on 152 sts.

Row 1 (right side):
Knit.

Row 2:
Knit.

Row 3:
K8, place marker; * † K2 tog; K2, YO, K5, YO, K2, sl 1,
K1, PSSO; K3, place marker †; K4, place marker; rep
from * 5 times more, then rep from † to † once; K8.

Row 4:
K8; * P16, K4; rep from * 5 times more; P16, K8.

Row 5:
K8; * † K5, K2 tog; K2, YO, K1, YO, K2, sl 1, K1,
PSSO; K2 †; K4; rep from * 5 times more, then rep
from † to † once; K8.

Row 6:
Rep Row 4.

Row 7:
K8; * † K4, K2 tog; K2, YO, K3, YO, K2, sl 1, K1,
PSSO; K1 †; K4; rep from * 5 times more, then rep
from † to † once; K8.

Row 8:
Rep Row 4.

Row 9:
K8; * † K3, K2 tog; K2, YO, K5, YO, K2, sl 1, K1, PSSO
†; K4; rep from * 5 times more, then rep from † to
† once; K8.

Row 10:
Rep Row 4.

Row 11:
K8; * † K2, K2 tog; K2, YO, K1, YO, K2, sl 1, K1,
PSSO; K5 †; K4; rep from * 5 times more, then rep
from † to † once; K8.

Row 12:
Rep Row 4.

Row 13:
K8; * † K1, K2 tog; K2, YO, K3, YO, K2, sl 1, K1, PSSO
†; K8; rep from * 5 times more, then rep from † to
† once; K12.

Row 14:
Rep Row 4.

Rep Rows 3 through 14 in sequence until piece measures about 52" from cast-on edge, ending by working a Row 14.

Next Two Rows:
Knit.

Bind off.

Fringe
Following Fringe instructions on page 8, make
Single Knot fringe. Cut 30" strands; use 2 strands for
each knot of fringe. Tie knots in each st across each
short end of afghan. Braid yarn from first 3 knots
together loosely, knot firmly to fasten, leaving 1"
ends. Continue braiding across fringe. Trim
ends even.

Am ric n

designed by Anne Morgan Jefferson, design courtesy of The NeedleWorks

Size:
About 56" x 72"

Materials:
Worsted weight yarn, 28 oz (1960 yds, 800 gms)
  blue; 17½ oz (1225 yds, 500 gms) each red and
  off white
Size 9 (5.25mm) straight knitting needles, or size
  required for gauge
Size 9, 36" circular knitting needle (for border)
Size 16 tapestry needle

Gauge:
4 sts = 1" in garter st (knit every row)

Instructions

Note: Entire afghan is worked in garter st. Leave a 10" end when beginning and ending a new color. Use these ends to sew squares together.

Each side border is worked separately on circular needles.

Square (make 48)

Triangle 1:
With off white and straight needles, cast on 2 sts.

Row 1 (wrong side):
Knit.

Row 2 (right side):
K1, inc (knit in front and back of next st)—3 sts.

Row 3:
Knit.

Row 4:
K1, inc; K1—4 sts.

Row 5:
Knit.

Row 6:
K1, inc; knit rem sts—5 sts.

Row 7:
Knit.

Rows 8 through 29:
Rep Rows 6 and 7 eleven times more. At end of Row 29—16 sts.

Row 30:
With red, K1, inc; knit rem sts—17 sts.

Row 31:
Knit.

Rows 32 through 45:
With red, rep Rows 6 and 7 seven times. At end of Row 45—24 sts.

Row 46:
With red, K2 tog; knit rem sts—23 sts.

Row 47:
Knit.

Rows 48 through 59:
Rep Rows 46 and 47 six times more. At end of Row 59—17 sts.

Rows 60 through 89:
With off white, rep Rows 46 and 47 fifteen times more. At end of Row 89—2 sts.

Row 90:
K2 tog. Draw up lp and cut yarn, leaving a 10" end.

Triangle 2:
Hold Triangle 1 with right side facing you and longest edge at top; with straight needles and blue, pick up 16 sts along first off white section, 15 sts along red section, and 16 sts along next off white section—47 sts (see **Diagram A**).

Diagram A

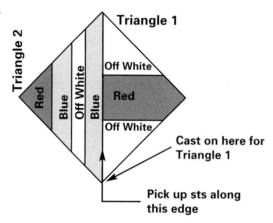

Row 1 (wrong side):
Knit.

Row 2 (right side):
K2 tog; knit to last 2 sts; K2 tog—45 sts.

Rows 3 through 12:
Rep Rows 1 and 2 five times more. At end of Row 12—35 sts.

Rows 13 through 20:
With off white, rep Rows 1 and 2 four times. At end of Row 20—27 sts.

Rows 21 through 32:
With blue, rep Rows 1 and 2 six times. At end of Row 34—15 sts.

Rows 33 through 44:
With red, rep Rows 1 and 2 six times. At end of Row 46—3 sts.

Row 45:
Rep Row 1.

Row 46:
Sl 1, K2 tog, PSSO. Draw up lp and cut yarn, leaving a 10" end.

Assembly
Step 1:
Make 12 large blocks by sewing 4 squares together with Row 48 of second triangles at center (see **Diagram B**).

Diagram B: 1 Large Block—4 squares sewn together

Step 2:
Arrange large blocks in four rows of three blocks each.

Border
Hold afghan with right side facing you and any side edge at top; with blue, pick up 30 sts along edge of each square.

Row 1 (wrong side):
Knit.

Row 2 (right side):
K1, inc; knit to last 2 sts; inc; K1.

Rows 3 through 32:
Rep Rows 1 and 2 fifteen times more.

Row 33:
Knit.

Bind off all sts as to purl.

Work border in same manner on remaining 3 sides.

With tapestry needle and blue, sew ends of rows together to form corners.

L zy Ri----in & H--lly

designed by Maureen Egan Emlet, design courtesy of The NeedleWorks

Size:
About 50" x 60"

Materials:
Worsted weight yarn, 42 oz (2880 yds, 1200 gms)
  off white; 3½ oz (240 yds, 100 gms) each red
  and green
Size 8 (5mm) 29" circular knitting needle, or size
  required for gauge
Size 16 tapestry needle

Gauge:
4 sts = 1" in stockinette st (knit one row, purl
  one row)

Special Abbreviation

M1 (make 1):
With left-hand needle, lift strand between last st
worked and next st on left-hand needle, purl—
M1 made.

Instructions
Loosely cast on 281 sts.

Row 1 (wrong side):
K5; * P1, (K3, P1) twice; K3, P7, (K3, P1) twice; K3;
rep from * to last 6 sts; P1, K5.

Row 2 (right side):
K5, sl next st as to purl, yf, sl same st back to left-
hand needle, turn, K5, turn, K5, yf, insert right-hand
needle as to knit under wrap and knit tog with next
st; * (P3, K1) twice; P3, K7, (P3, K1) 3 times; rep from
* to last 5 sts; K5.

Row 3:
K5, sl next st as to purl, yf, sl same st back to left-
hand needle, turn, K5, turn, K5, insert right-hand
needle from behind into back of wrap, place on left-
hand needle and purl tog with next st; * (K3, P1)
twice; K3, P7, (K3, P1) 3 times; rep from * to last
5 sts; K5.

Row 4:
K6; * P2 tog; P1, (K1, P3) twice; K1, M1 (see Special
Abbreviation); K5, M1; (K1, P3) twice; K1, P1, P2 tog;
K1; rep from * to last 5 sts; K5.

Row 5:
K5; * P1, K2, (P1, K3) twice; P1, K1, P5, K1, (P1, K3)
twice; P1, K2; rep from * to last 6 sts; P1, K5.

Row 6:
K6; * P2, K1, P1, P2 tog; K1, P3, K1, P1, K1, M1, K3,
M1, K1, P1, K1, P3, K1, P1, P2 tog; K1, P2, K1; rep
from * to last 5 sts; K5.

Row 7:
K5; * (P1, K2) twice; P1, K3, (P1, K1) twice; P3, (K1,
P1) twice; K3, (P1, K2) twice; rep from * to last 6 sts;
P1, K5.

Row 8:
K6; * (P2, K1) twice; P2 tog; (P1, K1) 3 times; M1, K1,
M1, (K1, P1) 3 times; P2 tog; (K1, P2) twice; K1; rep
from * to last 5 sts; K5.

Row 9:
K5; * (P1, K2) 3 times; (P1, K1) 6 times; (P1, K2) 3
times; rep from * to last 6 sts; P1, K5.

Row 10:
K6; * P2 tog; (K1, P2) twice; K1, inc (purl in front and back of next st) (K1, P1) 4 times; K1, inc; (K1, P2) twice; K1, P2 tog; K1; rep from * to last 5 sts; K5.

Row 11:
K5; * P1, K1, (P1, K2) 3 times; (P1, K1) 4 times; (P1, K2) 3 times; P1, K1; rep from * to last 6 sts; P1, K5.

Row 12:
K5, sl next st as to purl, yf, sl same st back to left-hand needle, turn, K5, turn, K5, insert right-hand needle as to knit under wrap and knit tog with next st; * P1, K1, P2 tog; (K1, P2) twice; K1, inc; (K1, P1) twice; K1, inc; (K1, P2) twice; K1, P2 tog; K1, P1, K1; rep from * to last 5 sts; K5.

Row 13:
K5, sl next st as to purl, yf, sl same st back to left-hand needle, turn, K5, turn, K5, yf, insert right-hand needle from behind into back of wrap, place on left-hand needle and purl tog with next st; * K1, P1, K1, (P1, K2) 3 times; (P1, K1) twice; (P1, K2) 3 times; (P1, K1) twice; P1; rep from * to last 5 sts; K5.

Row 14:
K6; * (P1, K1) twice; P2 tog; (K1, P2) twice; (K1, inc) twice; (K1, P2) twice; K1, P2 tog; (K1, P1) twice; K1; rep from * to last 5 sts; K5.

Row 15:
K5; * (P1, K1) 3 times; (P1, K2) 6 times; (P1, K1) 3 times; rep from * to last 6 sts; P1, K5.

Row 16:
K6; * K2 tog; (P1, K1) twice; inc; P1, K1, (P2, K1) 4 times; P1, inc; (K1, P1) twice; K2 tog tbl; K1; rep from * to last 5 sts; K5.

Row 17:
K5; * P2, (K1, P1) twice; K3, (P1, K2) 4 times; P1, K3, (P1, K1) twice; P1; rep from * to last 6 sts; P1, K5.

Row 18:
K6; * K1, K2 tog; P1, K1, P3, K1, inc; P1, (K1, P2) twice; K1, P1, inc; K1, P3, K1, P1, K2 tog tbl; K2; rep from * to last 5 sts; K5.

Row 19:
K5; * P3, K1, (P1, K3) twice; (P1, K2) twice; (P1, K3) twice; P1, K1, P2; rep from * to last 6 sts; P1, K5.

Row 20:
K6; * K2, K2 tog; (P3, K1) twice; inc; P1, K1, P1, inc; (K1, P3) twice; K2 tog tbl; K3; rep from * to last 5 sts; K5.

Row 21:
K5; * P4, (K3, P1) 5 times; K3, P3; rep from * to last 6 sts; P1, K5.

Row 22:
K5, sl next st as to purl, yf, sl same st back to left-hand needle, turn, K5, turn, K5, insert right-hand needle as to knit under wrap and knit tog with next st; * K3, (P3, K1) 5 times; P3, K4; rep from * to last 5 sts; K5.

Row 23:
K5, sl next st as to purl, yf, sl same st back to left-hand needle, turn, K5, turn, K5, yf, insert right-hand needle from behind into back of wrap, place on left-hand needle and purl tog with next st; * P3, (K3, P1) 5 times; K3, P4; rep from * to last 5 sts; K5.

Row 24:
K6; * K3, (P3, K1) 5 times; P3, K4; rep from * to last 5 sts; K5.

Row 25:
Rep Row 21.

Row 26:
K6; * K2, M1, (K1, P3) twice; K1, P1, P2 tog; K1, P2 tog; P1, (K1, P3) twice; K1, M1, K3; rep from * to last 5 sts; K5.

Row 27:
K5; * P3, K1, (P1, K3) twice; (P1, K2) twice; (P1, K3) twice; P1, K1, P2; rep from * to last 6 sts; P1, K5.

Row 28:
K6; * K1, M1, K1, P1, K1, P3, K1, P1, P2 tog; (K1, P2) twice; K1, P2 tog; P1, K1, P3, K1, P1, K1, M1, K2; rep from * to last 5 sts; K5.

Row 29:
K5; * P2, (K1, P1) twice; K3, (P1, K2) 4 times; P1, K3, (P1, K1) twice; P1; rep from * to last 6 sts; P1, K5.

Row 30:
K6; * M1, (K1, P1) 3 times; P2 tog; (K1, P2) 4 times; K1, P2 tog; (P1, K1) 3 times; M1, K1; rep from * to last 5 sts; K5.

continued

Row 31:
K5; * (P1, K1) 3 times; (P1, K2) 6 times; (P1, K1) 3 times; rep from * to last 6 sts; P1, K5.

Row 32:
K5, sl next st as to purl, yf, sl same st back to left-hand needle, turn, K5, turn, K5, insert right-hand needle as to knit under wrap and knit tog with next st; * (P1, K1) twice; inc; (K1, P2) twice; (K1, P2 tog) twice; (K1, P2) twice; K1, inc; (K1, P1) twice; K1; rep from * to last 5 sts; K5.

Row 33:
K5, sl next st as to purl, yf, sl same st back to left-hand needle, turn, K5, turn, K5, yf, insert right-hand needle from behind into back of wrap, place on left-hand needle and purl tog with next st; * K1, P1, K1, (P1, K2) 3 times; (P1, K1) twice; (P1, K2) 3 times; (P1, K1) twice; P1; rep from * to last 5 sts; K5.

Row 34:
K6; * P1, K1, inc; (K1, P2) twice; K1, P2 tog; (K1, P1) twice; K1, P2 tog; (K1, P2) twice; K1, inc; K1, P1, K1; rep from * to last 5 sts; K5.

Row 35:
K5; * P1, K1, (P1, K2) 3 times; (P1, K1) 4 times; (P1, K2) 3 times; P1, K1; rep from * to last 6 sts; P1, K5.

Row 36:
K6; * inc; (K1, P2) twice; K1, P2 tog; (K1, P1) 4 times; K1, P2 tog; (K1, P2) twice; K1, inc; K1; rep from * to last 5 sts; K5.

Row 37:
K5; * (P1, K2) 3 times; (P1, K1) 6 times; (P1, K2) 3 times; rep from * to last 6 sts; P1, K5.

Row 38:
K6; * (P2, K1) twice; P1, inc; (K1, P1) twice; K2 tog tbl; K1, K2 tog; (P1, K1) twice; inc; P1, K1, (P2, K1) twice; rep from * to last 5 sts; K5.

Row 39:
K5; * (P1, K2) twice; P1, K3, (P1, K1) twice; P3, (K1, P1) twice; K3, (P1, K2) twice; rep from * to last 6 sts; P1, K5.

Row 40:
K6; * P2, K1, P1, inc; K1, P3, K1, P1, K2 tog tbl; K3, K2 tog; P1, K1, P3, K1, inc; P1, K1, P2, K1; rep from * to last 5 sts; K5.

Row 41:
K5; * P1, K2, (P1, K3) twice; P1, K1, P5, K1, (P1, K3) twice; P1, K2; rep from * to last 6 sts; P1, K5.

Row 42:
K6; * P1, inc; (K1, P3) twice; K2 tog tbl; K5, K2 tog; (P3, K1) twice; inc; P1, K1; rep from * to last 5 sts; K5.

Row 43:
K5; * (P1, K3) 3 times; P7, (K3, P1) twice; K3; rep from * to last 6 sts; P1, K5.

Row 44:
K6; * (P3, K1) twice; P3, K7, (P3, K1) 3 times; rep from * to last 5 sts; K5.

Rows 45 through 308:
Rep Rows 1 through 44 six times more.

Bind off loosely.

Berry Clusters (make 13)
With red, cast on 1 st.

Note: Mark st through lower lp.

Row 1:
In st work (K1, YO, K1).

Row 2:
P1, in next st work (P1, YO, P1); P1.

Row 3:
K5.

Row 4:
P5.

Row 5:
K2 tog tbl; K1, K2 tog.

Row 6:
P3 tog.

Row 7:
Place unused lp of cast-on st (where marked) on needle, K2 tog.

Rows 8 through 21:
Rep Rows 1 through 7 twice more.

Bind off, leaving a 6" end.

Leaves (make 26**)**
With green, cast on 2 sts.

Row 1 (wrong side**):**
Purl.

Row 2 (right side**):**
K1, YO, K1—3 sts.

Row 3:
Purl.

Row 4:
K1, **(**M1, K1**)** twice—5 sts.

Row 5:
Purl.

Row 6:
K1, **(**M1, K1**)** 4 times—9 sts.

Row 7:
Purl.

Row 8:
Bind off 2 sts; K7.

Row 9:
Bind off 2 sts; P5.

Row 10:
Knit.

Row 11:
Purl.

Rows 12 through 17:
Rep Rows 6 through 11.

Row 18:
K1, sl 2 sts as to purl, K1, P2SSO; K1—3 sts.

Row 19:
Purl.

Row 20:
Sl 2 sts as to purl; K1, P2SSO—1 st.

Cut yarn leaving a 6" end; draw through rem st.

Finishing
With tapestry needle and long ends, randomly tack berry clusters to right side of afghan. Sew one leaf on each side of each berry cluster. Weave in all ends.

design courtesy of The NeedleWorks

Size:
About 40" x 56"

Materials:
Worsted weight yarn, 27 oz (1650 yds, 945 gms)
   lt grey
Size 10½ (6.50mm) 36" circular knitting needle, or
   size required for gauge
Stitch markers

Gauge:
16 sts = 3½" in cable patt
One full patt rep = 12"

Seed Stitch Pattern
Row 1:
P1; * K1, P1; rep from * across.
Row 2:
K1; * P1, K1; rep from * across.
Rep Rows 1 and 2 for seed st patt.

Cable Pattern
Row 1 (right side):
YO, K3, sl 1 as to knit, K1, PSSO; K11.
Row 2:
P10, P2 tog tbl; P3, YO, P1.
Row 3:
K2, YO, K3, sl 1 as to knit, K1, PSSO; K9.
Row 4:
P8, P2 tog tbl; P3, YO, P3.
Row 5:
K4, YO, K3, sl 1 as to knit, K1, PSSO; K7.
Row 6:
P6, P2 tog tbl; P3, YO, P5.
Row 7:
K6, YO, K3, sl 1 as to knit, K1, PSSO; K5.
Row 8:
P4, P2 tog tbl; P3, YO, P7.
Row 9:
K8, YO, K3, sl 1 as to knit, K1, PSSO; K3.
Row 10:
P2, P2 tog tbl; P3, YO, P9.
Row 11:
K10, YO, K3, sl 1 as to knit, K1, PSSO; K1.
Row 12:
P2 tog tbl; P3, YO, P11.
Rep Rows 1 through 12 for cable patt.

Bobble Stitch

In next st work (K1, P1) twice; turn, P4, turn, K4, turn, (P2 tog) twice; turn, K2 tog—bobble st made.

Lace Pattern

Row 1:
K13, YO, sl 1 as to knit, K2 tog, PSSO; YO, K13.

Row 2:
Purl.

Row 3:
K4 tog; (YO, K1) 5 times; YO, K4 tog; K1, bobble st; K1, K4 tog; (YO, K1) 5 times; YO, K4 tog.

Row 4:
Purl.

Row 5:
Rep Row 1.

Row 6:
Purl.

Row 7:
K4 tog; (YO, K1) 5 times; YO, K4 tog; K3, K4 tog; (YO, K1) 5 times; YO, K4 tog.

Row 8:
Purl.

Rows 9 through 11:
Rep Rows 5 through 7.

Row 12:
Purl.

Rep Rows 1 through 12 for patt.

Instructions

Cast on 175 sts.

Edging:
Rows 1 through 4:
Rep Rows 1 and 2 of seed st patt twice.

Body:
Row 1:
(P1, K1) twice; place marker; P2; * work Row 1 of cable patt over next 16 sts; P2; place marker; work Row 1 of lace pattern over next 29 sts; P2; rep from * twice more; place marker; work Row 1 of cable patt over next 16 sts; P2; place marker; (K1, P1) twice.

Note: Move markers as you come to them.

Row 2:
(P1, K1) twice; P2; * work Row 2 of cable patt over next 16 sts; P2; work Row 2 of lace patt over next 29 sts; P2; rep from * twice more; work Row 2 of cable patt over next 16 sts; (K1, P1) twice.

Continuing in patt as established and keeping 4 sts at end of each row in seed st, work until afghan measures about 55" from cast-on edge.

Next 4 Rows:
Rep Rows 1 and 2 of seed st patt twice.

Bind off.

Large Pillow & Afghan

designed by Linda Cyr, design courtesy of The NeedleWorks

Sizes:
Afghan: About 49" x 61"
Pillow: About 19" x 19"

Materials:
Worsted weight yarn, 39 oz (1755 yds,
   1105 gms) red; 36 oz (1620 yds, 1020 gms) black
Size 15 (10mm) knitting needles, or size required for
   gauge
Size N (9mm) crochet hook
18" square pillow form
Size 16 tapestry needle

Gauge:
10 sts = 4" in stockinette st (knit one row, purl
   one row)
12 rows = 4"

Instructions

Afghan
Note: Afghan is worked with 2 strands of yarn held together.

Strip (make 4)
With 2 strands of black held tog, cast on 30 sts.

Row 1 (right side):
K15; drop one strand of black; join one strand of red; with one strand of red and one strand of black, K15.

Row 2:
P15; drop red, pick up black; with 2 strands of black, P15.

Note: On Rows 3 through 18 when repeating Row 1 use red already joined.

Rows 3 through 18:
Rep Rows 1 and 2 eight times more.

Row 19:
Drop one strand of black, join red; with one strand of red and one strand of black, K15; drop black, pick up red, with 2 strands of red, K15.

Row 20:
P15; drop one strand of red, pick up black, with one strand of black and one strand of red, P14; pick up black, with all 3 strands, P1.

Note: On Rows 21 through 36 when repeating Row 19 use red already joined.

Rows 21 through 36:
Rep Rows 19 and 20 eight times more.

Rows 37 through 180:
Rep Rows 1 through 36 four times more.

Cut red.

Bind off, using 2 strands of black.

Assembly
Sew strips together, having all strips in same direction and carefully matching rows.

Finishing

Note: See Special Techniques beginning on page 5 for instructions on working single crochet stitches.

Hold afghan with right side facing you and cast-on edge at top; with 2 strands of black held together, make loop on hook and join with a single crochet stitch in first cast-on stitch in upper right-hand corner; work another single crochet stitch in same cast-on stitch; working around afghan, work a single crochet stitch in each st and in side of each row and work 2 single crochet stitches in each corner; join in first single crochet stitch.

Finish off and weave in ends.

Pillow

Note: Pillow is worked with 2 strands held together.

Front:

With 2 strands of red held tog, cast on 44 sts.

Row 1:

K15; drop one strand of red, join black; with one strand of red and one strand of black, K14; drop black, join another strand of red; with 2 strands of red, K15.

Row 2:

P15; drop one strand of red, pick up black; with one strand of red and one strand of black, P14; drop black, pick up red; with 2 strands of red, P15.

Note: On Rows 3 through 18 when repeating Row 1 use black already joined.

Rows 3 through 18:

Rep Rows 1 and 2 eight times more.

Row 19:

Join one strand of black, drop one strand of red; with one strand of black and one strand of red, K15; drop one strand of red, pick up one strand of black; with 2 strands of black, K14; drop one strand of black, pick up one strand of red; with one strand of black and one strand of red, K15.

Row 20:

P15; drop one strand of red, pick up one strand of black; with 2 strands of black, P14; drop one strand of black, pick up one strand of red; with one strand of black and one strand of red, P14; pick up 2nd strand of red; with 3 strands, P1.

Note: On Rows 21 through 36 when repeating Row 19 use black already joined.

Rows 21 through 36:

Rep Rows 19 and 20 eight times more.

Rows 37 through 54:

Rep Rows 1 through 36.

With 2 strands of red, bind off.

Back:

With 2 strands of red held tog, cast on 44 sts.

Row 1:

Knit.

Row 2:

Purl.

Rows 3 through 54:

Rep Rows 1 and 2 twenty-six times more.

Bind off.

Pocket:

Work same as for back through Row 28.

Bind off.

Finishing
Step 1:

Note: See Special Techniques beginning on page 5 for instructions on working single crochet stitches.

Hold pocket with right side facing you and bound-off row at top; with 2 strands of red held together, make loop on hook and join with a single crochet stitch in first bound-off stitch at right-hand edge; work one single crochet stitch in each remaining stitch.
Finish off.

continued

Step 2:
Hold wrong side of pocket to right side of back, matching sides and lower edges. With tapestry needle and 2 strands of black, sew a vertical seam up center to form 2 pockets.

Step 3:
Hold front and back pieces with wrong sides together, matching sides and lower edges; with 2 strands of black held together, make loop on hook and join with a single crochet stitch in right-hand corner through all 3 pieces. Carefully matching stitches, work single crochet stitches around three sides (spacing stitches so edges lay flat), working 2 single crochet stitches in each corner; insert pillow form; work single crochet stitches along 4th side; join in first single crochet stitch.

Finish off and weave in all ends.

Cable Stripes

designed by Melissa Leapman, design courtesy of The NeedleWorks

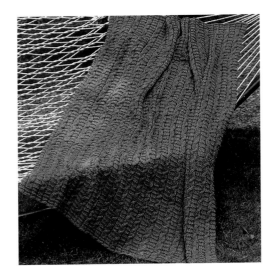

Size:
About 45" x 58"

Materials:
Worsted weight yarn, 42 oz (2184 yds,
    1470 gms) rose
Size 10½ (6.5mm) 36" circular knitting needle, or
    size required for gauge
Size 10 (5.75mm) 36" circular knitting needle

Gauge:
7 sts = 2" in stockinette st (knit one row, purl
    one row)

Instructions
With larger size needle, cast on 232 sts.

Change to smaller size needle.

Row 1 (right side):
Purl.

Row 2:
* P4, K2; rep from * to last 4 sts; P4.

Row 3:
K4; * P2, K4; rep from * across.

Row 4:
Purl.

Rows 5 through 12:
Rep Rows 1 through 4 twice more.

Change to larger size needle.

Row 13:
P4; * P2, K4, P6; rep from * across.

Row 14:
* P4, K2; rep from * to last 4 sts; P4.

Row 15:
K4; * P2, K4; rep from * across.

Row 16:
Rep Row 14.

Row 17:
P4; * P2, sl next 2 sts onto cable needle, hold
in back; K2, K2 from cable needle; P6; rep from
* across.

Rows 18 and 19:
Rep Rows 14 and 15.

Row 20:
Rep Row 14.

Rep Rows 13 through 20 until piece measures about
56" from cast-on edge, ending by working a Row 16.

Change to smaller size needle.

Next 9 Rows:
Rep Rows 1 through 4 twice, then rep Row 1
once more.

Change to larger size needle.

Bind off.

Bobbles on Point

designed by Sandy Scoville

Size:
About 40" x 50"

Materials:
Worsted weight yarn, 26 oz (1820 yds, 910 gms) natural

Size 10½ (6.5mm) 29" circular knitting needle, or size required for gauge

Gauge:
8 sts = 2" in stockinette st (knit one row, purl one row)

Pattern Stitch
Bobble:
In next st, knit in front, in back, in front, in back, and in front; turn, P5, turn, K5, turn, P2 tog; P1, P2 tog; turn, sl 1 as to knit, K2 tog, PSSO—bobble made.

Instructions
Cast on 181 sts.

Row 1 (right side):
Knit.

Rows 2 through 6:
Knit.

Body:

Row 1:
K6; * P4, K5, P4; rep from * 12 times more; K6.

Row 2:
K5, P1; * K4, P5, K4; rep from * 12 times more; P1, K5.

Row 3:
K6; * P3, K2 tog; K1, (YO, K1) twice; K2 tog tbl; P3; rep from * 12 times more; K6.

Row 4:
K5, P1; * K3, P7, K3; rep from * 12 times more; P1, K5.

Row 5:
K6; * P2, K2 tog; K1, YO, K3, YO, K1, K2 tog tbl; P2; rep from * 12 times more; K6.

Row 6:
K5, P1; * K2, P9, K2; rep from * 12 times more; P1, K5.

Note: The following two rows will lengthen the garter stitch borders, allowing more stretch.

Row 7:
K5, turn, K5, turn, K6; * P1, K2 tog; K1, YO, K5, YO, K1, K2 tog tbl; P1; rep from * 12 times more; K6.

Row 8:
K5, turn, K5, turn, K5, P1; * K1, P11, K1; rep from * 12 times more; P1, K5.

Row 9:
K6; * K2 tog; K1, YO, K3, bobble (see Pattern Stitch); K3, YO, K1, K2 tog tbl; rep from * 12 times more; K6.

Row 10:

K5, purl to last 5 sts; K5.

Row 11:

K6; * P4, K5, P4; rep from * 12 times more; K6.

Row 12:

K5, P1; * K4, P5, K4; rep from * 12 times more;
P1, K5.

Rows 13 through 20:

Rep Rows 3 through 10.

Rep Rows 1 through 20 until afghan measures about
49" from cast-on edge.

Rep Rows 1 through 5 once more.

Knit 6 rows.

Bind off.

Starlight

designed by Sandy Scoville

Size:
About 40" x 52"

Materials:
Bulky weight brushed yarn, 27 oz (1215 yds, 780
  gms) off white
Size 17 (12mm) 47" circular knitting needle, or size
  required for gauge

Gauge:
8 sts = 4" in stockinette st (knit one row, purl
  one row)

Pattern Stitch

Cluster (CL):
P3 tog leaving sts on left-hand needle; YO, purl
same 3 sts tog—CL made.

Instructions
Loosely cast on 107 sts.

Row 1 (right side):
Knit.

Row 2:
Knit.

Row 3:
Knit.

Row 4:
K3, P1; * CL (see Pattern Stitch); P1; rep from * 24
times more; K3.

Row 5:
Knit.

Row 6:
K3, P3, CL; * P1, CL; rep from * 22 times more; P3,
K3.

Rep Rows 3 through 6 until afghan measures about
51".

Next 3 Rows:
Knit.

Bind off loosely.

Fringe
Following Fringe instructions on page 8, make
Single Knot fringe. Cut 25" strands of yarn; use
6 strands for each knot. Tie knots evenly spaced
across each short end of afghan. Trim ends even.